SUPER
SANDCASTLE
State Stories

LENA AND THE LADY'S SLIPPERS

~ A Story About Minnesota ~

Written by Pam Scheunemann

Illustrated by Bob Doucet

Consulting Editor, Diane Craig, M.A./Reading Specialist

A Division of ABDO
ABDO
Publishing Company

visit us at www.abdopublishing.com

Published by ABDO Publishing Company, a division of ABDO, P.O. Box 398166, Minneapolis, Minnesota 55439. Copyright © 2011 by Abdo Consulting Group, Inc. International copyrights reserved in all countries. No part of this book may be reproduced in any form without written permission from the publisher. Super SandCastle™ is a trademark and logo of ABDO Publishing Company.

Printed in the United States of America, North Mankato, Minnesota
112010
012011

Editor: Liz Salzmann
Content Developer: Nancy Tuminelly
Cover and Interior Design: Anders Hanson, Mighty Media
Production: Colleen Dolphin, Oona Gaarder-Juntti, Mighty Media
Photo Credits: AP Photo/Paul Battaglia, Engbretson Underwater Photography, Great Lakes Aquarium, iStockphoto (Christopher Penler, Jenny Swanson), Laura Ingalls Wilder Museum, Walnut Grove, MN, Mall of America, Copyrighted and used with permission Mayo Foundation for Medical Education and Research, Mississippi Headwaters, ©2009 State of Minnesota, Department of Natural Resources, MN DNR Parks and Trails, reprinted with permission, One Mile Up, Quarter-dollar coin image from the United States Mint, Shutterstock, Thinkstock

Library of Congress Cataloging-in-Publication Data

Scheunemann, Pam, 1955-
  Lena and the lady's slippers : a story about Minnesota / Pam Scheunemann ; illustrated by Bob Doucet.
    p. cm. -- (Fact & fable: state stories)
  ISBN 978-1-61714-681-7
  1. Minnesota--Juvenile literature. I. Doucet, Bob. II. Title.
  F606.3.S38 2011
  977.6--dc22
                            2010022168

Super SandCastle™ books are created by a team of professional educators, reading specialists, and content developers around five essential components—phonemic awareness, phonics, vocabulary, text comprehension, and fluency—to assist young readers as they develop reading skills and strategies and increase their general knowledge. All books are written, reviewed, and leveled for guided reading, early reading intervention, and Accelerated Reader® programs for use in shared, guided, and independent reading and writing activities to support a balanced approach to literacy instruction.

TABLE OF CONTENTS

Paul Bunyan
(pg. 18)

walleye
(pg. 11)

Aerial
Lift Bridge
(pg. 17)

Bemidji

Duluth

Red River

Mississippi River

MINNESOTA

Mall of America
(pg. 12)

HALL OF AMERICA

common loon
(pg. 4)

Minneapolis

Minnetonka

St. Paul

showy lady's
slipper
(pg. 6)

Bloomington

Mankato

Rochester

Honeycrisp apple
(pg. 9)

LEGEND

⬡ CAPITAL   ◎ STORY START

○ CITY   - - - STORY PATH

~ RIVER   ✴ STORY END

Common Loon

The common loon is the Minnesota state bird. It lives on many Minnesota lakes. Loons spend most of their time on the water. They dive underwater to catch fish. The loon is known for its call. It sounds kind of like someone laughing.

LENA AND THE LADY'S SLIPPERS

It is early spring. Ole and Lena Loon are flying north. They had spent the long winter down south. Lena says, "We're back in Minnesota, Ole! Let's stop in Mankato and visit Goldie."

Ole wants a break. "Sure! I wonder how that little gopher is doing?" He also wanted to ask Goldie where to find some ladies' slippers for Lena.

Mankato

Mankato is in southern Minnesota. The Dakota Indians named it Mahkato which means greenish blue earth. A long time ago, there was a spelling mistake. It was never fixed, and Mahkato became Mankato!

5

Showy Lady's Slipper

The showy lady's slipper is the Minnesota state flower. It is illegal to pick or harm it. It can take 16 years to grow flowers. But it can live for 50 years!

Ole once heard Lena talking to Grace Graywolf about lady's slippers. Like most loons, Lena has a hard time walking on land. Ole thinks slippers might help! He wants to get Lena some for her birthday. But he just isn't sure where to find them!

At Goldie's, Ole whispers so Lena can't hear. "Goldie, do you know where I can find ladies' slippers for Lena?" he asks.

"Yes, there's a shoe store near Lake Minnetonka," replies Goldie.

"Thanks!" says Ole.

Gopher State

One of Minnesota's nicknames is The Gopher State. The Minnesota gopher is a thirteen-lined ground squirrel. It can be found throughout the state. The gopher is the **mascot** of the University of Minnesota's "Golden Gophers."

Lake Minnetonka

This is one of the largest lakes in Minnesota. It has many bays and islands. Minnetonka means "big waters" in the native Dakota language.

Ole and Lena wave good-bye to Goldie. "It was good to see you, Goldie!" they shout.

Lena's brother Sven lives on Lake Minnetonka. Ole suggests, "Lena, let's stop and see Sven."

"Okay. It's always fun to catch up with Sven," Lena says. Ole is glad she agreed. His plan is working!

Sven is happy to see Lena and Ole. He brings out some Honeycrisp apples for a snack. "It's been such a long time since I've seen you two. I should come up north this summer."

Lena smiles, "Come up anytime. The fishing is great!"

Honeycrisp Apple

The Honeycrisp apple was first grown at the University of Minnesota. Now it is grown in other states and around the world. It became Minnesota's state fruit in 2006.

Gray Wolf

There are about 2,500 gray wolves in Minnesota. They live in the northern half of the state. They travel in packs of 6 to 12. A wolf's sense of **smell** is 100 times stronger than a person's!

Meanwhile, Lena's friends are planning a surprise party for her! Willie Walleye, Grace Graywolf, and Mamie Moose find the perfect spot. There are lady's slippers everywhere. They know how much Lena likes them.

Everyone helps with the **decorations**. Mamie says, "Lena will be so surprised! Ole forgot her birthday last year. She was kind of sad."

"She won't have a thing to squawk about this year!" adds Willie Walleye.

Walleye

Minnesota's state fish is the walleye. It's named for its large, glassy eyes. The center of the eye **reflects** light. This helps the walleye see when it's dark underwater. Walleyes eat bugs and other fish.

11

Mall of America

The Mall of America opened in 1992. It attracts people from all over the world. It has more stores than any other mall in the United States. It even has an **amusement park**!

Back at Lake Minnetonka, Ole whispers, "Sven, do you know where I can find some ladies' slippers for Lena?"

"Try the Mall of America." Sven suggests.

"Good idea. Thanks, Sven. It won't be hard to get her to go to the mall!" Ole says.

After they leave Sven's, Ole says, "Lena, why don't we go to the Mall of America?"

Lena loves to shop so she agrees, "Ya, sure, Ole."

At the mall doors, Ole says, "Why don't we meet back here in an hour?"

"Sounds good to me. Then we can have lunch in Minneapolis!" Lena says.

Minneapolis

Minneapolis is on the Mississippi River. In the 1800s, lumber and flour mills were built near St. Anthony Falls. This helped the city grow. Minneapolis is nicknamed "The Mill City."

13

Mississippi River

The Mississippi is the second-longest river in the United States. It starts at Lake Itasca, in northern Minnesota. It flows all the way to the Gulf of Mexico. Some birds follow it when they fly north and south each year.

Ole finds some pretty ladies' slippers at a shoe store. He has them gift wrapped and sent to Grace for the surprise party. He meets Lena as planned, and they fly to Minneapolis for lunch. The **restaurant** is right on the Mississippi River.

Minnesota Wild Rice Soup

6 tablespoons butter

½ small onion, chopped

½ cup flour

3 cups chicken broth

2 cups wild rice (precooked)

1 cup sliced mushrooms

1 cup half-and-half

salt and pepper

Melt butter in a soup pot. Add the chopped onion. Sauté until soft. Stir in the flour to make a paste. Set the burner on medium heat. Slowly add the chicken broth. Mix with a whisk to avoid getting lumps. Add the rice, mushrooms, and half-and-half. Add salt and pepper to taste. Serve when hot.

Wild Rice

Native Americans have **harvested** wild rice for centuries. It is collected with a **canoe** and wooden sticks. One person moves the canoe with a pole. The other uses sticks to **knock** the **grain** into the boat. Wild rice is the Minnesota state grain.

They walk along the river to the **restaurant**. Lena says, "They have the best wild rice soup here. I love it!"

15

Duluth

Duluth is on the western point of Lake Superior. It began as a fur-trading settlement. Today Duluth is an important shipping **port** for the Great Lakes. Lake Superior's beautiful North Shore begins in Duluth.

After lunch Lena suggests a side trip to Duluth. For years they have wanted to see the Aerial Lift Bridge. Ole agrees, and they fly over the hills of Duluth. Lake Superior is quite a sight, shining in the sun.

"Ole," Lena **exclaims**, "it's beautiful! I'm so glad we came here!" They hear a ship's **horn** blowing.

Ole says, "Look, the bridge is rising. It's so cool!"

As the ship passes through, the horn blasts again.

"Sounds kind of like Aunt Gertie!" laughs Ole.

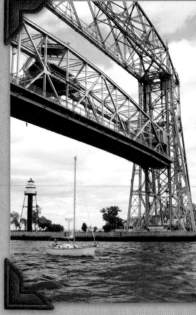

Aerial Lift Bridge

This bridge crosses a small **canal** between Park Point and Duluth. The bridge lifts so ships can pass through the canal. When the bridge is down, cars can drive over to Park Point. Some days, the bridge is raised more than 30 times!

17

Paul Bunyan

Paul Bunyan and Babe the Blue Ox are Minnesota legends. Tales of the giant lumberjack and his ox have been told for many years. Some say that Paul and Babe's **footprints** made Minnesota's 10,000 lakes!

Ole and Lena leave Duluth and fly west. Soon they see statues of Paul Bunyan and Babe the Blue Ox. "We're almost home!" says Ole.

Lena says, "Oh! I just remembered. Mamie Moose asked us to meet her in the park nearby."

"Oh, okay," Ole answers. The plan was working!

When Ole and Lena arrive, everyone shouts, "Surprise!"

"Ole!" Lena cries. "You remembered! Look at all the beautiful lady's slippers!"

"Ladies' slippers?" he asks.

"The flowers, silly!" Lena says. Then she opens Ole's gift.

Ole explains, "They're slippers for my lady!"

THE END

Land of 10,000 Lakes

Minnesota is called the "Land of 10,000 Lakes." But there are actually 11,842 lakes that are 10 **acres** (4 ha) or larger. Lake of the Woods and Lake Superior are the largest border lakes. Red Lake is the largest lake inside Minnesota.

19

MINNESOTA AT A GLANCE

Abbreviation: MN

Capital: St. Paul

Largest city: Minneapolis

Statehood: May 11, 1858 (32nd state)

Area: 86,939 square miles (225,171 sq km) (12th-largest state)

Nickname: Gopher State, Land of 10,000 Lakes, or North Star State

Motto: L'etoile du Nord — Star of the North

State flower: showy lady's slipper

State tree: Norway pine

State bird: common loon

State fish: walleye

State grain: wild rice

State butterfly: monarch

State song: "Hail! Minnesota"

STATE SEAL

STATE QUARTER

The Minnesota quarter shows a lake with Norway pines on the shore, two people in a fishing boat, and a swimming loon. There is an outline of the state with the nickname "Land of 10,000 Lakes."

STATE FLAG

WHAT DO YOU KNOW?

How well do you remember the story? Match the pictures to the questions below! Then check your answers at the bottom of the page!

a. slippers

b. Aerial Lift Bridge

c. Honeycrisp apples

d. Ole and Lena Loon

e. walleye

f. wild rice soup

1. Who is heading north in the spring?

2. What do Ole, Lena, and Sven have for a snack?

3. What kind of fish is Willie?

4. What does Ole buy at the Mall of America?

5. What does Lena have for lunch?

6. What do Ole and Lena see in Duluth?

Answers: 1) d 2) c 3) e 4) a 5) f 6) b

What to Do in Minnesota

1 ## Learn about Laura Ingalls Wilder

Laura Ingalls Wilder Museum, Walnut Grove

2 ## Explore a Cave

Niagara Cave, Harmony

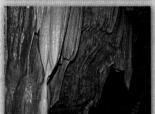

3 ## Take a Medical History Tour

Mayo Clinic, Rochester

4 ## Go to a Minnesota Twins Baseball Game

Target Field, Minneapolis

5 ## Tour the State Capitol Building

Minnesota State Capitol, St. Paul

6 ## Visit an Aquarium

Great Lakes Aquarium, Duluth

7 ## Take a Canoe Trip

Boundary Waters Canoe Area, Ely

8 ## See where the Mississippi River Begins

Itasca State Park, Lake Itasca

GLOSSARY

acre – a unit of measurement that equals 43,560 square feet (4,047 sq m). One acre is a little smaller than a football field.

amusement park – a place with rides, games, and other fun things to do.

canal – a man-made river that connects two bodies of water.

canoe – a narrow boat that has pointed ends and is moved using paddles or poles.

decoration – an item that is displayed to make something or someplace look festive or pretty.

exclaim – to speak with strong feeling.

footprint – a mark or track made by a foot or shoe.

grain – a seed of a cereal plant, such as rice or wheat.

harvest – to gather or collect crops.

horn – a device that gives a signal by making a loud noise.

knock – to hit something with force.

mascot – a person, animal, or object that is supposed to bring good luck to a team or an organization.

port – a body of water near land where boats come to pick up or drop off people or things.

reflect – to cause light, sound, or heat to bounce back.

restaurant – a place to buy and eat a meal.

smell – the ability to sense an odor or scent.